Despatch Note

702-3760400-6857036

Order Number 702-3760400-6857036 **Supplied by** More4U Books & Music

Catalogue Number	Title and Artist	Qty
= 9781479768301	The Dance Macabre (New Edition): (New Edition) [Ha	1

SOME ITEMS MAY BE SHIPPED SEPARATELY

Order Processed: 07/10/2016 15:01:

Payment has been received from: Rev. Deborah Foster

RETURNS: Return the item with this despatch note to the following address: Paperbackshop.co.uk Ltd, Unit 22 Horcott Industrial Estate, Horcott Road, FAIRFORD, Gloucestershire GL7 4BX, UK. Please tick one reason for return: 1. | | Damaged 2. | | Faulty 3. | | Wrong Item 4. | | Other
Would you like: a refund | | a replacement | |

The Dance Macabre
(new edition)

The Dance Macabre
(new edition)

Book Two

(Paean on the nature of life and death as a Humanist Philosophy)

Herein begins the tale of life and death
The Dance Macabre: a poem
Imagomortis

All souls live but one brief lifespan, take beauty from this fact, endeavour through the power of love to offer with thine acts, to aid all living creatures, for their suffering be Man's.

Steven Parris Ward

To order additional copies of this book, contact:
Xlibris Corporation
0-800-644-6988
www.Xlibrispublishing.co.uk
Orders@Xlibrispublishing.co.uk
305637

All souls live but one brief life span,

Take beauty from this fact,

Endeavour, through the power of love,

to offer with thine acts,

To aid all living creatures,

For their suffering be Man's.

Herein lies book two of the epic poem . . .

The Voyage of Life

(a poetic trilogy that details the rebirth of a man)

Herein begins The Voyage of Life (a trilogy which details the rebirth of Man)

From dust thou came to dust return borne on the stellar winds, Let spirit to the source return and be reborn again, to sing in passionate praise of how our life force shall remain.

wherein resides . . .

The Dance Macabre

(Paean on the nature of life and death as a Humanist Philosophy)

"Dance Macabre" is a generic term often used for a variety of artistic expressions concerning the universality of death. Irrespective of one's station in life, the "dance of death" unites all. The following epic poem may be linked to a historic tradition found in many cultures: for Danse Macabre (French), Danza Macabra (Italian and Spanish), or Totentanz (German), were late-medieval allegories which invariably represented a personified Death leading a row of dancing figures to the grave; typically with an emperor, king, youngster, and beautiful girl in the entourage. The intention of such tales and images reminds people of how fragile their lives are, and how vain are the glories of earthly life.

Preface

What is the poet's task? First, with the utterance and music of their verse, the poet creates a lyrical expression of their own inner thoughts and feelings. Thus, the poet gives voice to the music of the personality or "soul". As such, it is a psychological as well as a creative process; as it represents the personal process of "individuation". Here, the artist not only strives to attain a catharsis of his or her unexpressed emotions, but also attempts to bring into a unity the disparate elements of their own soul (manifested as emotion and reason). They achieve this through the practice and crafting of an expressed form.

The interior process of creativity might well be one where the artist invokes a kind of interior prayer: a continuous repetition of the words and verses, which thereby reduces the inner self to a state of order, or a more unified psychological harmony. In this, the poet practices a form of hesychasm; an interior repetition of the poetic mantra, so as to induce a psychological change within. The poet creates a personal expression of their inner self; a psychological and emotional map of their own thoughts, dreams and aspirations. Here, poetry becomes an expression of the poet's personal cosmos, or an expression of the inner process of ordering the self.

The oral recitation of a poem is the poetic cosmos given form by the rational logos of the poet's utterances. In this, the poet adapts the role of a kind of shaman, or hero; a psychic intermediary (or medium) between the audience and the inner visions, claimed by some to be divine or other worldly. The shaman poet, largely through oral recitation, gives access to the hidden labyrinths of the mind. In this, poets evoke both reason and emotion in other individuals, and offer images of inner worlds to produce a response. The response for individuals, therefore, might well induce a catalyst for their own interior psychological *harmonia;* as well as acting as an inspirational catalyst to create further poetry in turn. This reflects a circular argument, as well as a creative act.

In the beginning was the word, and the word was with God. And God *said* let there be light, and there was light. These Biblical passages, amongst others, express the creative process of God, and the power of God as the creative Logos—the Reason or *the Word* of creativity. For believers, God produces the order of the cosmos, and this Logos or Reason gives birth to, and eternally sustains, the cosmos. Such a cosmic creative act has parallels in the poetic enterprise. For humanists, however, this is not a divine truth received from God, but a literary and poetic expression. An expression of inner visions based in the realm of the *human* imagination. As such these parallels serve only to emphasise the metaphoric and literary content of the Bible as poetry, and its place therefore requires it to be contextualised as a testament to the power of the human imagination, not as a received truth from a beneficent other worldly deity, as Christians might profess it to be.

The duty of the poet is twofold: First, to help the individual and thence humanity; for without love for the individual, there can be no common fellowship, or notions of self-improvement for the world community. Second, to attempt to articulate the big questions which underpin the thoughts and feelings of the human soul. These universal concerns unfold within the content of The Dance Macabre. To whit: What is the purpose of life? Is there a God? Is there an immortal soul? What constitutes living the good life? What are the injustices and perils which we face in the world, and must overcome, in our efforts to develop free and improving democratic constitutions? What constitutes our understanding of this universe? To address some of these issues, I have utilised the emotive power of both religious and scientific imagery, in order to create an allegory of the human soul, and through this chartered a psychological journey of one man's attempt to understand himself in relation to the universal.

In its overall form The Dance Macabre represents the passage from life to death and the inevitability of such a process, whilst serving as a poetic memento mori. Its aim, however, is not to denigrate or pour scorn on the value or beauty of life. In this, it does not communicate a negative vision empty of meaning, but offers a persuasive reminder of the importance of living this life to the full, free from the fear of death. In this, it does not shirk the problems of religious belief, nor does it take refuge in them. It does not seek to quell such fears, by promulgating faith in the myth of a loving and beneficent deity, where salvation can be found. It has rather been my concern to offer a poetic paean of praise to the beauty and value of this cosmos. A view free from the notions of a conscious, omnipotent, invisible creator deity, active in human affairs. In doing this, the clarion call is for mankind to take responsibility for its own actions, to stand above the superstitions of past archaic beliefs, to exercise its rational powers, whilst not denigrating the intuitive or emotive qualities which make us human beings. In order to integrate these qualities, and to value the worth of humankind, I have emphasised the importance of striving to improve humanity for its own sake, and for all living forms, by emphasising the importance of the philosophic life, and focusing on contextualising soul in the cosmic process. Here mankind, and the appeal to improve our understanding of the environments which we inhabit, both ethical, social, terrestrial and universal, take centre stage.

The Dance Macabre offers the archetypal image of the angelic muse Urania; a muse imbued with various virtuous and cosmic characteristics. Urania is first an astronomical and celestial Muse. In this she is a representation of the cosmos as a whole, and in this she also symbolises unity. She is not Spirit itself, but a representation of Spirit. An archetypal symbol, but not the archetype itself. As such, she symbolises that force that combines all aspects of the cosmos, and she symbolises that which causes it to be.

Soul is a product of the life energy of Spirit in conjunction with organic bio matter. As a causal principle, Spirit is envisaged fundamentally in photonic terms, as those particles, or bundles of energy force, which cause various elementary particles to arise and unite, and hence ultimately organic life to live and breathe. Spirit has no personality, or conscious notions of action in itself. It is purely the unity principle. That which causes photonic energy to produce, through collision pair production, the various particles (electrons and positrons) which come to constitute the matter of the cosmos, the stars, and indeed the elements which constitute the human body. In this then Spirit unites, and in conjunction with matter causes the life consciousness of the soul to arise; facilitating awareness and unity with the cosmos. This energy makes inanimate matter dynamic, and is manifest through movement and life actions. Embodied, it is the causal energy for thoughts and feelings, and it assists the Voyager to develop towards psychological integration: uniting the anima and animus, the masculine and feminine principles of the soul.

As a manifestation of Spirit, Urania is also the symbol, as Muse, that facilitates poetic creativity through her presence. In this, she facilitates within the soul the higher faculty of the Imagination; a faculty which causes creativity. It is the faculty which arises from the combination of both reason and the emotional faculties. In facilitating the creative process, she is a source of life and light. Yet she also represents unity of process. Both the process of psychological transformation, but also of the cosmic process. As such she is in a continuing state of flux, evolving and ever changing. She symbolises, as a unity, the combination of conflicting aspects of soul, but she also represents the cosmic process, of life and death; for this is inextricably combined with all aspects of the cosmos as a process bound to organic forms.

The journey then can be interpreted on a variety of levels, all equally pertinent. Each canto might be seen as the death throes of the body and soul as Spirit is released. In this death experience, the journey, which the Voyager undertakes, might be viewed as a process of self-discovery before death. A process where the various and sometimes disparate faculties of the self become integrated through Urania's presence. In another respect, Dance Macabre represents interior conversations with the various faculties of the Voyager's own self. Thence, as he evolves towards unity, he meets the King—who represents the egocentric passions—and the Voyager, who is represented by the, as yet, disunited rational and emotional faculties.

Regarding the characterisation of these attributes of soul, the work represents an interior monologue, and as such it does not follow the conventions of traditional speech punctuation. In another respect, the Voyager's conversations can be viewed as the individual's progression from ignorance to understanding, from differentiation (where we see ourselves apart from our global environment, as something other) to a unity. The process of attempting to achieve unity, on an individual and collective basis, offers purpose and meaning to our lives. It promotes personal awareness, assures our continuing evolution, and it contextualises our place in our evolving notion of cosmos.

SPW 2012

ark ye souls who recite or read with heartfelt sympathy, and know this song that I oft writ wrong, did arise from my faculties, The Spirit Great did the soul create, but my soul writ poetry.

Canto One

*The Voyager meets his Muse whilst on this journey known as life,
and passes through the spheres of change deemed by Necessity.*

*Midway on the voyage, 'twixt birth to death, I lost my way,[1]
So set myself a timely quest, a noble path to tread,
Of liberating my true self from all the ties that bind,
Through reason more than faith,
that through this method I would find,
A way of purging life from all desires which cause distress,
So I might pass beyond the veil-
to realms of emptiness.[2]*

*I was not burdened with a heavy heart upon the quest,
For I had never sought a life of indolent content,
Or treasured all those things that others held to be of value,
My pride did boast I once believed I'd lived my life by virtue;
In truth I was, however, so much farther from that goal,
Blinded by the sin of pride and worldly arrogance.*

*Upon the course, one moonlit night, I took a path ascending,
Where moss thick grew, enclosed around, with bough and bracken dense,
The mists arising slow did hang, as blackness swift enfolding,
Did feed my fear to offer up a prayer to Providence.*

---

[1]   Allusions to Dante's Inferno. Lack of one syllable to denote "loss". "twixt birth" - 4 beats, balanced- "to death" (Hence in the middle). "I lost" (in the middle) "my way". "lost" lacking 1 syllable of "the voyage".

[2]   Śūnyatā, Sanskrit noun from the adj. *śūnya*: "zero, nothing"), *Suññatā* (Pāliadj. *suñña*), *stong-pa nyid* (*Kōng/Kū*, 空 (Chinese/Japanese), *Gong-seong*, 공성(空性) (Korean), *qoyusun* (Mongolian), is frequently translated into English as *emptiness* or *thusness*. The theme of emptiness (*śūnyatā*) comes from the Buddhist doctrines of the nonexistence of the self (Pāli: *anatta*, Sanskrit: *anātman*) and dependent origination.

The thorn and twisted branch did catch. Strange spectre forms appearing,
Did force me from the chosen path that I did strive to take,
Until I foundered blind upon a space, a rocky clearing,
To witness with my senses sounds which round did emanate.

If in my mind, or all around, I flit, anticipating,
The source of where those cadences of sound did true belong,
They filled the air with dreams, my breast did pound, as unabating,
My pulse and raw emotion sought that portamento song.

My breath I held in gaping fear, as choirs resonating,
Did mix within the rhythm of my breath, I stood aghast,
Till soul and body now estranged, my legs did turn to shaking,
As there before I recognised a sight I could not grasp.

Descending from the ether, in the heaven realms unbounded,
In clouds of glory streaming, and in rays of shimmering light,
Angelic forms, a crystalline bright halo there surrounded,
And in that aura radiant, perfection met my sight.

My erring soul did there perceive a vision of a Lady,
Celestial her outer form, a glittering effluence,
As I then thought I did behold the bless`ed Virgin Mary,
Who stood alive before me, devout and luminous.

Two roses on her feet around her ankles were entwin`ed,
Her raiment like the silver stars, her girdle shone like gold,
Her hair as white as driven snow did fall and flow refin`ed,
She was the true and perfect One made manifest and whole.

Within the very centre-point adorned by bless`ed beauty,
I did behold a countenance that put all sin to flight,
Which woke within my consciousness a stronger sense of duty,
To acquiesce to her, and serve with all my strength and might.

I was bereft of speech and thought, in this thus brought to reverence,
As I beheld this image and light-portal from the skies,
I knelt before her presence lost in fear and humble deference,
Before her graceful hand did show the sign that I should rise,
And indicated then that I need have no fear of vengeance,
She did not Lord Jehovah's wrathful anger thus evoke,
But with great love, compassion, spoke with grace and placid patience,
A sacred consecration,
which she in my heart awoke.

(Muse):
Fear not thyself I am thyself,

A thousand rushing winds,
Did issue from my inner being,
as though each were a tongue,
Of living incandescent flame, revealing visions sacred,
Angelic signs,
That struck me blind,
And paradisic songs,
the truth of which in human words be inexpressible.

(Muse):
Fear not thyself and know thyself,
Oh mortal man behold!
To witness through thine eyes the revelations of the soul.

In speaking this she did not utter sounds of mortal nature,
But entered through a doorway to a chamber in my mind,
And there she dwelt invoking love, a close communicator,
Dispensing truth and other worldly prophecies refined.

(Muse):
Be glad that space and time my love,
retreats to distant ages,
To free you from all sorrows to
a life reborn anew.
Come forth now from your mortal shell,
as Spirit rearranges,
In garments golden, braided with
the wealth of heaven true.

As she, this song of silence sung, my soul became refin`ed,
Or purified, I know not which, my mundane faculties,
And all the dregs of former wrongs did die, my eyes were blinded,
My naked soul thence twice released from all the ties that bind.

And by this she did truth impart, befitting of her station,
My soul became as one with her, true comfort I did find,
And in that state of love and grace her blest illumination,
Was thence transferred, so that we both shared body, heart and mind.

(Muse):
I am by life and Spirit formed,
to be your Muse, Surrender,
The Great Unknown hath made me,
Shown, as guide to light the way.
The human mind could never span the compass of that splendor,
I am the force to lead you forth,
beyond all thought mundane.

A wave of fear then rose within, eclipsing my devotion,
As I did question openly the substance of her being,
For if the form before me did transcend thought and emotion,
My soul must have run riot,
Crazed, and conjured up this dream,
To fill my mind with devil's thoughts and strange imagining.

(Muse):
To see is a reflection shown, by sense as a deception,
A vision or a dream which is not real, but is confined,
Within the fixed perimeters of reason and perception,
which yet transcends all forms of life and being of that kind.

Fear not, submit, invoke not dread, and offer no resistance,
There be no peace in waging war, or joy in inner strife,
Take my embrace, be glad, and learn the nature of existence,
Upon the wandering journey that reveals the voyage of life.

And as my Lady took me by the hand she softly whispered,
As then my soul transmuted to another sphere refined,
Ascending as photonic light,
As space and time extended,
My soul endured catharsis,
And full slipped the links that bind.

(The Voyager):
I shall Urania name thee,
My sacred guide acclaim thee,
Great Muse, my spirit portal,
Transcending joy immortal.

Pure visions be thy token,
Gifts by the soul now spoken,
All living truth re-telleth,
With Evas' name re-spelleth.

All sin and fault repressing,
The truth be thy great blessing,
Free now the worldly-minded,
Illuminate the blinded.

Fair Maiden, gentle, lowly,
Kept singularly holy,
Purge now the sins that bind me,
Instruct so I might know thee.

Chorus:

Dance now and lead thy brother,
For he shall praise no other,
To yield by supplication,
And sense each intimation.

Evoke through visions waking,
The force of divine making,
Which death and life be joined to,
By Spirit, breath and fortune.

Thy gift shall then be given,
The spirit merge with heaven,
Until new life be woken,
No circle shall be broken.

Thence Spirit's force be married,
By soul and body carried,
New Life from death ascending,
With Spirit never ending.

Canto Two

The Muse then deems to show her power with wondrous transformations. Therein discussed the nature of the cosmic confluent; its manifest and latent forms, and sacred affectations, and how they bear relation to life, death and punishment.

As I then with my Lady did survey the plains of Eden,
My thoughts expelled did rest upon her countenance divine,
Her heavenly gaze did through her eyes communicate her beauty,
Which introduced the first of many icons to my mind.

Transported back to reason through her ever guiding presence,
My mind through thought did first perceive a vision in her eye,
As I beheld a poet pale that formed from out the essence,
Whose face did yet retain the light and nature of my guide.

The rose lipped poet spoke his words as I in rapt attention,
Did contemplate their meaning and their true significance,
Beguiled by every nuance and the craft of his invention,
I smiled with pleasure at his simple poem's elegance.

(The Poet):
Beauty bound by heaven's powers,
Though glorious be but nought if our,
Fair souls be blind to nature's bowers,
Be glad and praise each stone and flower.

For in life's symmetry apparent,
Fair nature shares her joy transparent,
In wonder through that light concurrent.
How splendid shines her love recurrent,

Reveal'ed root and vein'ed leaf,
The starlit laden night replete,
Each part shines out, effulgent glows,
With glorious, radiant light on show.

The comet with its plumage bright,
Shall orbit 'fore it then departs,
Be led 'pon wings in stellar flight,
Ejected from the solar heart.

The vistas of the galaxies,
Reveal in awe and majesty,
The One's noetic qualities,
Betrothed to time and space.

And in the twilight of the morn,
As crimson mantled sun ascends,
And we aspire to view the dawn,
To witness as a loving friend:
Do not forget that at our feet are wonders still as great as these,
We too may hold within our hands,
Precious infinity.

Within the whorl of sunflower seeds a galaxy may be perceived,
Within the song of morning break the music of the spheres,
And as the dying embers burn, our hearts inspired shall gladdening turn,
Towards the sun, that orb of light, that caused this world to be.

Be of good cheer, my dearest friend,
Fear not the night, 'tis not the end,
Ill fortunes bear and grief amend,
Be kind of heart, no sorrows send.

For brief is life and life unspent,
Be wasted without pure intent,
Too much our hearts in anger vent,
Too few through love their hearts present.

(The Voyager):
If animate complexity,
Is not designed as God's good dance,
but came to be eventually,
by circumstance and cosmic chance;
Is there no principle or plan?
Is what I see just what I am?
Is life and death the fate of man?
To live and die,
and then decay?

The poet gazed towards the sun now setting in the west,
As if such questions once he'd raised, and used men's faith to test,
In times long past, when he had sailed upon the earthbound seas,
And dared to question God as being a true necessity.

(The Poet):
Heaping hearts with scorn and ire for life's complexities,
Disguises truth which oft be found in life's simplicities,
Seek not a heavy burden to consign upon your brother,
Who finds life hard and troublesome enough, yet finds in succor,
The milk of human kindness, and the trust to still believe,
That human beings are more than just the sum of what they see.

Through love and deeds we strive for peace, and by this mark we measure,
Not natural laws but miracles,
through Christ men have endeavored,
To find the gift of paradise,
and immortality.

Such is the Christian dogma, and by this priests have men bound,
To keep their minds and thought and words free from all blasphemies,
And keep their tongues free only for the speech of holy sounds,
Although in truth I do confess despair in such beliefs:
For how can God who loves all things condemn his son to die?
If he be just and love is pure?

He looked up to the sky,
As if he was addressing an irrational deity.

We found ourselves disputing then the theme so oft debated,
That God divine makes rules and laws, and is the cause creative,
And dutifully exerts a power upon our destinies.

(The Voyager):
Through miracles, the Bible claims, God's powers may thus be shown,
And through such acts doth God use men,
So that his will be known,
Communicated, it is claimed, through prayer and love to save,
The wretched sinners on this Earth from the perils of the grave.

Yet if it be forbidden that men break the natural laws,
Conferred by God as just laws based on His experience,
God should desist from miracles, lest they reveal His flaws:
For holy acts should not trespass His natural influence.

Above all else God must provide true measure by his grace,
To set the right example of how all mankind should act,
He cannot seek to make the rules of nature yet replace,
His sacred laws with miracles,
lest virtue be displaced.

(The Voyager continues):
If 'God' exists is nature just the process of its Mind?
Or is God just a dream of men's creative influence?
Or is the truth that God exists and causes in men's lives,
A cosmic order far beyond derived coincidence?

(The Poet):
This cosmos is an order true and in its sanctity,
Replete with life and measure lies unfathomed mysteries,
But all contained within its sphere embodies harmony,
And all that acts must therefore act for Good eventually.

And thus from Good arises Form and from that source the sun,
Which causes life to replicate. to thrive and multiply,
And thus the chain of being emanating from the One,

Ensures that all that lives and breathes and moves shall never die.
And none of this a God requires to rule or justify.

Chorus:
Oh science great do not berate the mind that still believes,
In Spirit's power, reveal'ed in good nature's parity!

The poet then did seek to calm in offering his faith,
When witnessing the strange concern which spread across my face.

(The Poet):
Be not afraid my dear good friend,
This is no time to steep,
Your mind in dread uncertainties, or lose untroubled sleep,
For in the deepest valley, cave or snowy mountain peak,
Upon the crowded city streets, or here in twilight's gloom,
There dwells a piece of heaven's light,
A flame that burns eternal,
There is a spirit immanent,
Which lives beyond the tomb.

I asked the poet earnestly, with all polite sincerity,
To tell me how we could believe in this dichotomy?
I asked the poet once again, with growing doubt to justify,
And clarify the nature of the mortal and divine.

Are bodies formed as temples, where immortal souls reside,
Proclaimed as holy essence,
or mere figments of the mind?
Are we consigned to life designed, expelled from out the womb,
To live one life as mortal, die, thence rot within the tomb?

If elements in truth house not eternal sparks divine,
Is God, as Soul, a fiction?
Or is fiction, truth misaligned?
And if it be a fiction placed,
And God by lies defaced,
What be the purpose of this life for virtue's state of grace?

Should we partake of all the wicked pleasures of our time?
Or spurn good virtue's temperance,
break the bread, and drink the wine?

(The Poet):

Such myriad problems I confide,
Once greatly weighed upon my mind,
Live life and love, and don't deny, life's pleasures brief is my reply,
For those who cannot find in God a reason to believe.

So that when death at last awaits,
We can with conscience clear abate,
The fear of our mortality,
and die with equanimity.

But faith proclaims a Spirit, which transcends our errant sins,
A Spirit force, which binds the cosmic body, life to give,
A virtuous Cause creative that bears life and soul within,
A spark of life, that causes soul to move, and matter live.

That spark of life that through desire doth cause all things to act,
This is the mystic nature of the holy marriage pact,
The binding of that force makes soul that causes all we see,
'Tis matter joined with Spirit which reveals this mystery.

And I believe with all my heart to this we shall return,
Beyond this life, our spirits strive for this, and truly yearn,
To be united with this cause, as lovers long to be.

I mused upon the poet's words, but found no consolation,
Within my heart and mind his words mere discontent provoked,
I wondered if the claims he made were simply affectations,
Until he with a voice assured,
a synthesis invoked.

The Poet speaks as Urania:

The Good which is the template of all matter manifested,
Revealed as perfect order shall exhibit certain laws,

As cosmos it communes, and by the Good it is reflected,
As virtue in the physical; an icon of the cause.

Arising from the birth and generation of all matter,
Great Spirit forms the body, thence the body makes the soul,
Preceding from the elements, united when once scattered,
The Soul, once born, doth yield the mind, Great Spirit binds the whole.

As living forms are born to die, the nature of existence,
Determines all must bear the shadow of mortality,
But when the atoms dissipate, causality's persistence,
Ensures that life is new reformed by their affinity.

And formed from stellar matter, which evolves through countless ages,
We cannot live apart, for every atom makes the whole,
Each living form, which is reborn, shaped by successive stages,
Might then contain the essence of a universal soul.

(The Voyager):
In this I am the atheist, which you once claimed to be,
Distributing your pamphlets and defending liberty,
You shunned the theological and spoke of anarchy,
Espoused the nature of all life more biologically.

There is no Soul Creator which the priests believe is given,
No truth be had in making God a Soul divinity,
Embrace the virtue of mankind without the blinds of heaven,
Affirm the humanistic creed, and soul's mortality.

The Poet smiled and nodded at the matters I'd disclos`ed,
By priests and men of piety who'd spurned the view he'd shown:
That Spirit was indeed the cause, and by that force enclose`ed,
And thoughts of God producing souls could not be borne alone.

I then discussed the Poet's claim that in the final moments,
Our life force joins The Great Good Source, yet not one soul shall be,
By vengeful God, cruel punish`ed, a wrathful Judge of Judges,
Or drown,
lost in the burning depths

of raging fiery seas.
And yet within these claims I found his thoughts ambiguous.

For if this world,
the countless planets, galaxies and stars,
By virtuous emanation form exactly as they are,
To state, within the cosmos great, that wickedness persists,
Appears to be in rational terms a strange hypothesis;
For how can something evil thus derive from something good?
And how can that which causes this be viewed beneficent?

(The Voyager):

Goodness' emanation should the fruit of sin desist,
Yet evil imperfections born by nature do exist,
And with such imperfection value judgements oft are made,
But made by erring judgement,
it be wrong to think God saves,
Good soul's from Hell's damnation,
flaying bodies to the grave.

(The Poet):

Theistic sham assumptions, how can souls once dead be saved?
If mind or soul cannot endure beyond the rotting grave,
For souls are life and consciousness that live within the form,
Which is the human body,
With emotions it adorns,
Impelling inert matter to its actions, dreams and thoughts,
within the chambers of its heart and mind throughout the course,
Of this, the journey known as life.
'til death life must withdraw.

The process of this chemistry, must be when life expires,
the factor which shall terminate the personality;
For death denotes the end of that brief physical formation,
Which caused the sorrows and the joys of mental perturbations.

Thus due to this, our mortal minds, which are of Nature born,
May have no need to thus berate great Goodness as the source,

For every fault and error, which has natural consequence,
Derives from birth, or nurture, borne by nature's influence.

(The Voyager):
Yet if great evil in the world exists without a name,
Then that which caused all things to be,
must surely take the blame,
Accepting this the Spirit Cause cannot be wholly Good,
And God if Good, who acts to judge,
has marred beneficence. [1]

(The Poet):
It may in truth be that the Spirit seeks to yet evolve,
By measure to another which first caused all life to be,
It may in truth be that the guilt of men be not involved,
in that which yet absorbs us in its perfect symmetry.

(The Voyager):
Is this then God, this Spirit great, which animates all matter?
I asked the question quizzically, as he did raise a smile,
It may well be
he vague replied, uncertain, as he answered,
Before his thoughts preoccupied, did form more poetry.

(Poet):
Spirit is unconscious,
As an ocean or a sea,
And in it thrives all moving souls,
which live and breathe and be,
within its flowing currents caught, like fish beneath the waves,

---

[1] For as the Good itself must surely measure laws and norms, then that which should be good and true, deriving from that form, should not be thought to thus negate such virtuous influence: no God should then an evil show in wrathful punishments, unless it be like humans limited in virtue blessed, and if that be what right is deemed that it should be addressed, by that superior title which fair justice then requests?

we breathe until the ebb returns,
To take us to the grave.

The Cosmic Force unites all things,
And causes minds to see,
but yields no jurisdiction,
That exceeds causality,
It causes mortal life and soul as conscious faculties,
yet shall persist forever when from bodies it be free.

Whilst vengeful Gods and other myths,
Turn free men into slaves,
Curtail the happy spirit and the courage of the brave,
We two must cleave to virtues for by these good truth inspires,
And act in fair accordance with the truth of our desires.

With such desires, I did proclaim the rights of anarchy,
The war of revolution, and the claims of liberty,
Both marital and spiritual, I sought to break the chains,
Which bound the country of my birth, and forced the free be slaves.

Yet retributive punishments, for wicked acts contrived,
Are punishments inflicted, yet unworthy of the crime,
They are no more of benefit than ignorance designed;
Let not a human be condemned for showing ignorance.

Punishment of sinful acts, immoral retribution,
Exacts a sense of justice and a timely recompense,
But only yields more blood from blood in any constitution,
Reforming education then must conquer ignorance.

Error is a measure based on human calculation,
And limited perceptions of the Good and noble Forms,
Such shades cannot approach the truth of virtue's emanation,
For all of these perceptions held fall short of Goodness' norm.

Yet let men strive through knowledge to achieve a better measure,
And strive to match such virtues living free and morally,

Such virtues acted through their lives are worth more than the treasure,
Of gold or jewels which men might gain, but lose eventually.

(The Poet changing back to the Muse):
To realise the nature of the truest liberty,
All souls must live the good in life, endeavor honestly,
To practice through their minds and hearts divine philosophy,
That practice, which embodies Good, shall truly set you free.

No prison formed from time or space shall cause you to be bound,
Or be a silent witness to the truth that sets souls free,
Address the sights before you, which within you now are found,
Condemn such retributions, and the verse of blasphemy.

The Muse then metamorphosised,
into a man I recognised,
And there within her depthless eyes,
there gazed a noble Florentine,
Of fifty years or more I guessed,
and laurel kissed his brow.

But I could not my conscience keep,
within my soul my ire did speak,
To give plain voice to those who seek,
the truth within the stars.

(The Voyager):
Oh Dante Alighieri, thou failed to read the signs,
By justifying muthos as a true philosophy,
Using superstitious fear, to poison good men's minds,
With circles within circles in a foul complexity.

A muthos is a tale believed which lacking reason favours,
Fantastic tales which oft belie good reason's influence,
It seeks to preach religious lies, yet pious souls endangers,
Assigning faith a precedence, whilst feeding ignorance.

Philosophy,
the champion of all verbal disputation,

Shall furnish keys to put an end to mental slavery,
The dialectic stepping stones support investigation,
Through science and induction, liberates methodically.

Oh Dante Alighieri, you propagated lies,
Supporting through your mythic Hell a Church theology,
Suggesting that the wrath of God extended from the skies,
And vengeance passed in Hell occurred without a court or trial,
Whilst claiming divine justice lay in retributive pain.

If Hell in truth, be Satan's realm, that lacks God's divine presence,
And God's great power doth not extend to places less divine,
The power of God is limited, it be not omnipresent,
And Satan then exacts the price, and sinful souls refines.

But why would He, who has no cause, such sinful errors punish?
Or be concerned to seek revenge—injustices revise,
if Satan doth embody sin, and sin seeks to encourage,
Shall Evil love not evil acts, but evil then despise?

But Satan too is punish'ed, whilst froze in silence, chained,
Devouring undigested souls in Hell, thou sought to claim:
Because he tried to steal from God the glories of His name,
Proud potency bred vanity; Thence God exacted pain.

"Each sin committed on the Earth in Hell in due proportion,
Affords a measured punishment, befitting of the crime",
Yet lives of sin, some seventy years, must be a grave distortion,
To earn eternal punishment dismissive of the time.

If Minos be the great Greek king ensuring proper censure,
Then why a pagan arbiter doth Dante then select?
If pagan spirits are assigned the justice and the measure,
Almighty God remits, and thence is guilty of neglect.

Oh Dante Alighieri, thou failed to read the signs,
Across the years, you festered fears, to nurture hateful crime,
That caused the humanistic creed to wither on the vine,
Converted by the Church's needs to bloody politics.

Oh Dante Alighieri, thou peddled superstitions,
The sinful crimes that did derive the Spanish Inquisition,
You laid a blind foundation false that silenced and confined,
The noble Galileo's voice, whose theories were decried.

The Spanish Inquisition did your mythic work condemn,
As blasphemous, corrupt and false, along with innocents,
But from that stance they did react with ruthless diligence,
Perpetuating torture from a base of ignorance.

As ignorance breeds ignorance; a continuity,
They justified, as you did too, unending misery,
By unjust trials, although your mythic work did seek to shame,
The Holy Church, and all that sought to profit from God's name.

To ravish men with poetry persuading men to see,
That wickedness of pleasures, and the politics of greed,
Corrupted good men's tempers, life and fair society:
That was your just endeavour and your happy policy.

But punishing those favoured ill, in lurid fantasies,
Promoting brutish tortures for their infidelities,
Imbues the truth of torture with a false reality,
Suggesting pain can benefit, pollutes the sanctity,
Of all that men hold sacred,
if they value dignity.

Canto Three

The Muse with grace, a third form shows; revealed a poet painter,
who speaks with ardent passion of his fair love Beatrice, until she
doth instruct upon a newer inspirateur, and how from joy and sorrow
it transcends inspiratrice.

I realised this voyage of life,
with all its pains and pleasures past,
Was more than just a play, or craft,
to merry God's amusement.

So too, I knew the Muse's task,
would shape more ghosts so I could grasp,
The weaknesses of those now passed to quicken my resolve.

Thence with these thoughts I sought to keep,
From off my mind the reign of sleep,
And kneeling meek, I offered up
a prayer of supplication.

(The Voyager):
Oh Spirit—let my life pass not in idled hours unlettered,
Resolve the sacred task in me, so I might find the sense,
and courage to explain in verse this dance of life unfettered—
free from the curse of puerile words,
With virtue's diligence,
Help me to write the truth, to purge the stubborn mind's pretence.

And not for wealth or glory great, shall I recite this journey,
As in the laboured depths of night, I wrestle with the facts,
Envisaging elusive words, my heart and mind extended,
With hope, to find your grace and love, to guide me to the task,
So that I may communicate thy loving ways at last.

My guide revealed another form, as I did ponder on,
And there revealed a broken man, weighed down by love, bereft,
To prompt my mind to broad reflect,
How strange be nature that projects,
all of its beauty, but elects,
to spurn fair virtue's intellect:
For if the soul a body makes,
Should not the body thence partake,
Of all the fair and noble traits,
collected by the soul?

My Lady's sacred silence orchestrated no reply,
Yet in that dearth, plagued not was I, with dour uncertainty,
But strengthened by her grace, and by such faith, which she assigned,
My joyous soul inclined to trust, and reasoning declined.

The poet painter's voice then spoke,
And through his words a chorus broke,
To ornament his past regrets, with pity's sorrowed sounds.

(Painter):
I knew a child of yore, who graced by Beauty's hand didst turn,
In youth, to venture forth, Spoke I to her,
of all my heart's affections.
Thence wrought with passions great, refined by love, I sorely yearned,
To capture her, my truest heart, through craft,
with all my skilled invention.

To praise my muse, Ophelia,-
Who offered violets fair,[1]

---

[1] Ophelia says in Hamlet "I would give you some violets, but they withered all when my father died. They say he made a good end." For Claudius she gives her fennel and columbines. Fennel stood for flattery, such as a king would receive and such that Claudius would give. Columbine was also a symbol of infidelity in love. To the queen and herself, she gives rue. Rue stood for sorrow and repentance. Ophelia distinguishes which meaning is for whom, when she says "you must wear your rue with a difference". It is obvious that she means repentance for the queen and sorrow for herself. A daisy, also for the queen, stood for deception in love affairs. The last

Crafted I such icons through the lustre of her hair,
And from her smile seductive she gave tongue, in verse I lingered,
Whilst she didst draw sad music from taut strings with agile fingers.
To wake in me such memories of distant voyages past,
She plucked a golden dulcimer,
Which in her hands she clasped.

Thence she, from girlhood grown, drawn pure as was the Blessed Virgin,
Shown an angel; which didst speak to her in dreams of Godly love,
With much devout and sincere faith did rest as woman prayed,
To hark her sacred angel's song at night,
she tender did abide.

As one devout until her time assigned,
She kept the merits of her grace confined,
And by good duty kept her charm and place,
With silence borne upon her loving face.

Till on her Beauty illness' pallor crept,
With shadowed songs of Death which marred her strength,
Whilst she poor fitted to Earth's realms was sent,
God's strong desire her spirit to repent.

Grave maladies, which from her body seemed,
To hasten that made purer by her heart,
Gave up in verse her longing to her dreams,
As like a daimon yearning to depart,
the earth—Confined—her spirit sought to roam,
There to alight 'pon heaven's sacred throne.

---

flowers she mentions are violets. Violets stand for faithfulness. It is likely that this allusion is made with regards to Hamlet since Laertes called Hamlet's affections a "violet in the youth of primy nature". It is perhaps Ophelia's own interpretation that Hamlet's faithfulness has withered and she cannot possibly love him again.

From this with anguish issued, shed by tears, he did reflect,
Upon the consequences of his dead wife's sad neglect:

Oh Beata, Fair Beatrix, the heaven's blaze, my child,
You woke a life shamanic, with the absence of your smile.
My love endures, but sweet recourse, could ne'er thine body save,
Now empty hollows form thine eyes,
made worm feed for the grave.

Chorus:
Beata mea domina!

The painter proud, berated then, No happiness he shared,
His rue and deep assurance ran, with pained conviction free,
He ran the gauntlet of his ire, his joy for love compared,
With common folk, who stoke`d not, Love's creativity:

Of those poor souls, who know not joy, by patronage of beauty,
Their hearts and minds, alack define, they fail to empathise,
Through love adjudged, bare they the drudge, through dull, domestic duty,
Touch not the stars, great heaven's bars,
Through Beauty recognised.

Beata mea domina!

Through children borne, they may pass on, nature's heredities,
Through offspring, bear their gift; a share of immortality,
But mortal love, bears not the gift, of Art's true sacred name,
Knows nought of that eternal bliss, her chasten`ed kiss ordained.

Beata mea domina!

How great the work artistic is, that draws from human forms,
The grace of perfect womanhood, her beauty thrice adorned,
With lilies three, within her grasp, [1]

---

[1]   Calla Lilies represent elegance, charm, beauty and grace, and are for a sophisticated
touch. The Madonna Lily is a symbol of purity, the white ones being associated with

Blest by the rose of heaven,
A robe ungirt,
from clasp to hem,
And numbered stars of seven.[1]

Beata mea domina!

My Lady thence, her thoughts gave voice, in measured tones of song,
Recounting love, by artist's shame, as error, right or wrong.

(The Muse):
With flowing lines, and vines in bloom, entwined around her shoulder,
You captured her fair titian hair, a crown for glory's name,
Her raptured face—in spaces still, rich robes didst soft enfold her,
The painter's song, ten kisses long, her passionate love refrain.

Time passed in years, the bowers, fears, kept hid in private places,
Love's laughter gone, long silence filled the chamber, empty shared,
No more embraced by heaven, joined in marriage, bound by labour,
The growing fullness of her time didst come, but birthed not fair.

---

the Holy Virgin by Christians. Christians believe that the lily had been yellow until the Virgin Mary picked it up. Lilies are a symbol of fertility, being used as a wedding flower, and also of death, being placed on graves. It is said that lilies spontaneously appeared on the graves of people executed for crimes they did not commit. Dreaming of lilies in spring signifies marriage, happiness and prosperity. Dreaming of lilies in winter signifies frustration of hopes and the premature death of a loved one. In medieval times, lilies symbolized feminine sexuality.

[1] The Blessed Damozel leans out from the outermost boundary separating heaven from space. Her eyes are deeper than the bottom of still waters. In one hand she holds three lilies attesting to her purity and the nearness of the triune God. In her hair are seven stars symbolizing the Pleiades, the seven daughters of Atlas and Pleione in Greek mythology. Included are Alcyone, Celaeno, Electra, Maia, Merope, Sterope, and Taygete, who attended the goddess of virginity, Artemis. After they died, they suffered the usual fate of those the God's favoured by becoming stars in the heavens. The open robe has affixed to it, a single white rose, a gift of the Blessed Virgin Mary in recognition of the damozel's faithful service to Heaven. She is thrice adorned as Beauty in womanly form, in heaven, and upon the canvas. Recalling Plato's distinction of art being a copy twice removed from the reality of the Forms.

You ne'er decried, thou yet denied, her love its freedom harboured,
You strove for fame, rich trappings, clung, desired too ardently,
The old refrain, once more you sang, But through a wreck less ardor,
You sullied love, with oils and blood-
Your bloodline vanity:

Speak not whilst in the presence of my sister,
Speak not whilst sat upon the model's chair,
Speak not to show your lack of school'ed learning,
Court silence sweet, my blessed damozel fair.

When she had lost her child and mystic beauty,
She through her pain still suffered for your art,
When she did need good love as true affection,
You yet refrained, to break her gentle heart.

In cultivating art in faithful service,
You pledged your troth and sold all that you framed,
But then soon sought out other lips to worship,
Yet found her face recaptured once again.

In seeking courtly love, your passion wandered,
She was but one of many that you met,
In reverence to the greater quest you favoured,
A host of graceful muses to beget.

You once did pause upon life's passing journey,
To sing her praise to fill the empty space,
How sweet the verse that once adorned her beauty,
How swift a book of poems is displaced.

At this, the painter's head, low bent in sorrow at this shame,
To hide his weakness, suffering, his eyes bore not to weep;
Before He spoke sincere, of how, by former love's refrain,
Each tender smile he'd cherished, but love's virtue failed to keep.

(Painter):
We once held court with love in private places,
In streets and houses spoke in tender tongues,

But life too soon did sketch the bitter traces,
Of loss reflected in our words and songs.

A lady fair, once blessed me with her favour,
And I the knight of old did seek her charms,
She graced me with her love, but yet I wavered,
To leave the love and comfort of her arms.

In seeking courtly love, my passion wandered,
She was but one of many that I knew,
Too soon my lady's trust and love I squandered,
A host of graceful muses sought anew:

A queen in opal, or a saint, an angel with a sword,
Not as they were, but as she was, when she was still adored.

For I was weak, my legs were wax,
My mind was made of flesh,
I scattered all my fertile seed,
But harvested regret.

Yes I was weak, my legs were wax,
My feet were made of clay,
Writ now within my House of Life,
Is death, dust and decay.

At this his voice began to fade, His face and form erase,
But as it slipped from consciousness, my Muse's voice conveyed,
A closing psalm to part, and mark the dawning of the day:

Hold sacred that all living things in Nature,
Have equal worth and common qualities,
Treat those you know as loving friends and neighbours,
And place not those fair faced beyond degree.

All selfless love in duty doth embody,
The sacred, and it gladly gives recourse,
Cosmetic beauty is a passing favour,
And as the years shall pass, shall run its course.

Instate no one below your class or station,
Take not your pleasures if and when you can,
To fuel the fire of pride yields cold aloofness,
Extinguishes the brotherhood of Man.

Canto Four

*The Voyager is transported by his guide to foreign shores,
and there berates the Foolish King's idea of rule and laws. Upon
this shore the deeds of war are argued and attacked, before Urania
intercedes to clarify the facts.*

*The tapering beams of early morn did warm alight on Eden's shore,
And signified that I should now (accompanied by my guide),
Not tarry on this holy site,
But swift pursue the depths of night,
We rose aloft in wing`ed flight
and fled the breaking dawn.*

*The sea did roar, the waves did roll,
The spray did salt the tongue,
The phantom flags on distant ships upon the masts were hung,
No sleep did steal the seaman's eyes, or rock his cradled brain,
As the howling wind did lash the course, lost sleep had changed her name,
From sweet repos`ed dreams of home,
to a bitter death refrain.*

Here continues the tale of the Fourth Canto

he driving rain, the tattered sail,
The moaning creaking deck,
The looming waves like mountains fell,
And caused one ship to wreck,
Upon some deadly hidden reef,
Whilst my spirit did protect,
My fragile soul from all real harm and mortal
frailties.

The driving rain, the tattered sail,
The moaning, creaking deck,
The looming waves like mountains fell,
And caused one ship to wreck,
Upon some hidden deadly reef,
whilst my spirit did protect,
My fragile soul from all real harm,
and mortal frailties.

Across the raging tempest blasts, we braved the ocean's icy clasp,
Until like mariners lost we gasped,
Then breached upon the shore.

Breathless from the last endeavour, I did kiss the earth,
Submitting to my pacing heart,
Whilst my Spirit did observe,
With placid curiosity, as I in gratitude,
Sought solace from the trembling night with sleep's restorative.

Oh Sleep,
who doth entwine the soul with shrouds of still repose,
Who dwells with lengthening shadows on the boundaries of the day,
Thou lends with thine extended arm a measure that beholds,
The truth of dreams, before the mind awoke, is led astray.

Thou knows best how to marry with that suitor named the Night,
For Light incites the mind with too much strange activity,
Night teeters on the brink of sight, and lulls the mind with Sleep,
To harbour Day's illusions which our wandering memories keep.

Though dreams oft flit like phantom forms,
Across the inner eye,
They bear a new dimension,
By their rich reality,
Invoking through their vividness a strange disparity,
They come to waking consciousness not how they true should be.

For dreams portend the future,
But are fragments of the past,
Forgotten expectations,
Of our lost experience.

And dreams hold forth their precious gifts,
But too soon draw away;
Their treasures shown, thence stolen
by the dawning of the day.

Amidst the breaking light of morn I then awoke to see,
Before my weakened, sleep filled eyes, a living effigy:
And there within an august tomb,
upon a throne of marble sat,
A frowning statesman proudly hewn,
From out the rock with skill and craft.

His name engraved was Abraham,
Whilst serfs did wait at his right hand,
In groups of four by his command,
He there discussed his wicked plans,
To reign in fear in many lands.

Once in his country's ardent youth,
Great pilgrims toiled to write the proofs,
Their testaments for guiding truth,
in noble constitutions.

They sought to save men from such lies,
That tyrants use to justify,
The merits of why thousands die,
Their spirits now are needed.

I knelt before this deceased king, unconscious of the fact,
That through his mouth the present king did speak and think and act.

(The Foolish King):

I am the King of this domain,
Who speaks of rights in freedom's name,
And all who question or refrain,
Shall feel the dread and awful pain,
My bloody fist,
Their spirits tame,
For guns and war be my chief aim!

I am upon a holy quest,
to free the tortured and oppressed,
From madmen who might act the fool,
I swift shall vanquish them to rule.

The justice found through freedom's gain,
Shall overcome the loss or pain,
Of those who die or worse be maimed,
Whilst guns and war shall seal my fame.

Achieving through my fearful might,
The guiding law of wrong from right,
Requires an iron will in war,
I love the weak, and loathe the poor.

I scare the strong and love the meek,
As countries quake beneath my feet,
I spread the tidings glad that all,
Shall benefit from freedom.

A liberty where all can buy,
an ethic which swift nullifies,
the masses, and thus pacifies,
All credible objections.

'pon bended knee, and humble posed, I asked before the fact,
If he could tell me in whose name he justified such acts?

(The Foolish King):

In God's name son, He sanctions,
I often hear His voice,
So blest are my grave actions,
as He speaks through each choice.

(The Voyager):

Is man or God the measure that determines wrong or right?
And how can God's opinion rule in a democracy?
If king's be deemed the measure true,
as you perceive the light,
God's will must be determined as a cruel theocracy,
And by your hand you instigate that rule through tyranny.

I then recalled that Lincoln,
meditating on such claims,
Once showed the weakness of them, and such errors to men's shame:

Can God's great will in truth prevail, in every deed or act?
If two conflicting parties claim to act by His desire?
For both may be, or one must be, oblivious of the fact,
And one must thence relinquish claims, that they God's will enact.

Wise men and women live their lives by measuring their visions,
With counsel drawn from fellowship,
discussion yields the proof,
Through godly claims, one man may rule,
which boosts his own opinions,
But one who rules in tyranny,
is no Guardian of the Truth.

The frowning statesman answered then in deep exultant tones,
And issued proclamations of his next desired campaign,
Reading from his manuscript, alighted on his throne,
He spoke of war, and all the spoils and pleasures he could claim.

(The Foolish King):
Who would deny that I the King should march throughout the captured streets,
And hail my conquered subjects with a strong and grave salute?
Upon the vanquished throne I'll sit,
and call my counsels' call for peace,
foolhardy, as I strategise my next triumphant battle.

Peace shall not quench my heated blood,
I long to slay with flaming swords,
all those who will not hail my name,
and to my will be pliant.

Give me the map, so I might find,
the next and choicest foreign clime,
And soon all countries shall be mine,
and be my prized possession.

Princes, Statesmen, Caesars, Tsars, and all of great humanity,
Shall come to worship at my feet and beg for my advice,
Thence I shall them bestow with grace,
if they shall bow and know their place,
And punish those who please me not with swift, remorseless vengeance!

From this I knew that he who perched upon that kingly throne,
Acquired the garb and title proud, but was in truth a sham,
Whilst treating men as puppets and his ministers as drones,
He knew not fellowship with God,
Nor brotherhood of Man.

(The Voyager):
You are no President of God.
You are not Abraham!
You are a cruel dictator,
Who destroys with evil plans.

My timid voice did muster strength, as I with fortitude did seek,
the affirmation of my charge,
my gracious comforter.

As she did nod a single time, my courage strengthened keen,
so I no longer felt compelled to rest 'pon bended knee,
But stood as all men should upright, and took my timely gaze,
Upon the face of he who stole all interests for his name.

(The Voyager):
Though men should seek to prosper from the victories they have gained,
No king should seek to wage a war for power, wealth or fame.
No man, or King, or President should seek to overrule,
The mandate of the people's will,
unless he be a fool!

The King with narrowing gaze did spit a bitter reprimand,
At this outrageous comment,
That besmirched his regal stand,
And as he drew a gasp of breath he sought to rectify,
The merits of his well-staged plan by meeting eye with eye.

(The Foolish King):
Be silent chimp, and know your place!
Do you dispute the fact?
That I alone do wield the truth,
and through a higher pact,
commune with God,
and therefore know precisely how to act.
Whilst you are but a common drone,
I represent the truth,
which justifies my role as Chief,
based on my inner proofs!

My bless`ed reason then did seek to timely intercede,
And with good sense relieve the King of Godly fripperies.

(The Voyager):
A mandate from the people,
needs a separate Church and State,
to stop mad Kings or Presidents,
who claim to know the weight,
And letter of the law is best determined by their measure,
Derive no power in Godly claims,
or claim that courts should ever,
Concede their power to whims or wiles, or trumped up justices.

(Muse):
One truth apparent, men free hold, as sacred and divine;
that all are born as equals, with the right to speak their minds,
based on such measured narrative, they shall this right define,
and bearing laws they shall espouse,
Their oaths and acts inclined:
To keep the preservation of this life through liberty,
To safe guard human happiness,
And keep their country free.

But Foolish Kings are deaf and dumb, and Foolish Kings be blind,
They hear just what they wish to hear, and spurn all counsel wise!

The Spirit's spoke, lamenting, but the words she did impart,
no favour found, he sat unmoved,
Whilst in his soul and heart,
He listened to his voice of God, which he himself had conjured,
To justify the merits of his great inequities.

The Foolish King did then extend a gnarled and knotted finger,
As if his skill and cunning from his mind he sought to flex,
And banish or extract within me any doubts that lingered,
By adding to each word and thought a stronger emphasis.

(The Foolish King):
No man or woman would accept my ransom at a price,
Accept a war of profit waged,
Or meet a rich king's vice,
But listen boy
(the King did hiss with unrestrain`ed glee),
I'm not the fool that you in anger make me out to be,
For I devised, with some great men, a better strategy,
To elevate the baseness of my war's inequities.

(Counsellor):
It shall ensure great profits for his ailing industries,
So that the greater good might be achieved eventually!

(King):
Imagine if, one bright clear day,
around the start of Fall,
A cruel and hideous crime took place,
which woke conviction's call.
Upon the very land which I, in peaceful company,
Had sought to rule with justice, and designed sincerity.

A band of men who killed for God, yet fought against the king,
Would through a plot to maim and kill,
Destroy most everything,
Which symbolised, my wealth and power, which caused my country's freedom,
And by that act, I would enact a long protracted war.

No obstacle within their path would stop the cruel endeavour,
For at that time my forces would be busy in the West,
So that their cruel atrocity would always live forever,
Within the minds of citizens,
they should not fail their test.

Counsellor:
We'd help them carry out their crime with true duplicity.

King:
Like hammers falling from the skies to shake the towers' construction,
They would swoop down upon their helpless prey from out the heights,
Condemning many innocents by force of the destruction.
To quicken those survivors left to fight the greater fight,
To call for arms in sorrow, and to flex my nation's might.

Imagine what an outrage there would be at such an act,
Senators would sympathise,
and sign to any pact,
Which I or my good colleagues thought might stem the threatening tide,
And all within the bless'ed name of more security.

The safety of my people, and a message plied with fear,
Would curb all criticism, 'til the world would bend an ear,
I'd nod my brusque approval, and with slogans shake my fist,
Of the need to slay with purpose all the evil terrorists.

All this achieved, it would then be a fairly easy task,
To ask my loyal subjects to re-launch my battle crafts,
To seek the orchestrators, who had planned to kill and maim,
By instigating war abroad, to catch the one's we blamed.

(The Foolish King):
Consider now the profits that would surely come about,
A princely sum of millions would be claimed without a doubt,
The war's expenses would be met, collecting taxes fair,
The country swift invaded,
once the target was declared,
The terrorists would scatter, whilst the leaders paid the price,
And I would claim the oil reserve, a war spoil for the heist.

My private armies, ready stand, awaiting to ensure,
That every whim of my command shall make the war endure,
Claiming by my power and arms more valued territory,
I shall ensure more profit through a war of parity.

In truth it does not matter if the country fits the crime,
If they be wicked sinners any country which may lie,
Towards the East may serve to be the sacrificial lamb,
If it be rich, and full with oil, I'll wage war if I can.

And if I rid the people there of monster and dictator,
Who ruled with ruthless tyranny, and murdered kith and kin,
Then all so much the better,
It will fortify my venture,
And lend a moral ethos to enforce my wish or whim.

As you perceive my higher aim rests not on fame or glory,
Or profit which would there arise from grateful circumstance,
I have the education of the people first for surely,
The virtues of our culture must be given every chance . . .

Counsellor (suggesting as the king stutters):
To wipe their minds of all the horrors of their recent past?

King (nodding dismissively):
I do this for the greater good to keep hegemony,
That all shall know the wonder of the ethics of the free,
And with our rich advantages a global territory,
Will be carved out, and all rogue states destroyed eventually.

Counsellor:
All those who speak may be a threat,
And may be thus detained,
Detract the Habeas Corpus writ to punish without pain.

(Voyager):
A government, if it be just, the moral ground should claim,
No government, if it be right, should torture, kill or maim,
If democratic law be just, bide not such travesties,
Lest people in their outrage, start a battle for the free.

Chorus:

A foolish king who claims he rules as God through jurisdiction,
To override the law, and good democracy displace,
A tyrant is who hides the truth of fairness through conviction,
This man who has no right to wear a smile upon his face,
Whilst others on the fields of battle bleed to prove his case,
Your oath of office and your lies are more than a disgrace.

Mad king, who spins as hypocrite, who lies, and justice hides,
You too should be arrested, and convicted of war crimes,
Detained and then imprisoned by the power of sword and shield,
For you have never served upon the noble battlefield,
Nor would you risk your life or limbs, whilst by your tyranny,
You mouth your strong convictions with a sick hypocrisy.

At this the Muse then touched my robe and with a calming hand,
Prepared my soul to journey on to witness other lands,
Whilst offering my grieving heart a noble benediction,
To quieten my solicitudes and bolster my convictions.

(Urania's Blessing):

Bless`ed be the peacemakers, who do not sorrow bring,
The death of war, or poverty, to any living thing,
Bless`ed be the pure in heart, who labour to achieve,
Justice and equality, they toil not to receive,
But seek to bring to those in need,
the strength to pacify,
the sorrows of the suffering,
with hope they change the lives,
Of all who bear the pain and loss of war and poverty,
And through their great endeavours,
they perfect humanity.

Good citizens, please find the strength to stand by your convictions,
And know the constitution as original testament,
Imperfect is but apt to change,
permit but one restriction:
No tyrant king must mar or spoil this great experiment.

Emancipation is not born without the bloody hand,
In this good men once died to form the sacred union,
Let not their names thence be defiled, invading foreign lands,
Let wars be fought for freedom, not pre-emptive profit plans.

Though Kings be great, no Chief of State should rule an institution,
Or choose to wield war principle's, to keep the upper hand,
True democratic principles, require a constitution,
Expressive of the people's will,
before a sole command.

Remember too, though kings be great, so many lose their station,
And many fall from giddy heights through their disparity,
With people's hopes, which form the very bedrock of a nation,
Those dreams of change should bring about a better legacy.

Then in my heart my Lady spoke, to strengthen with compassion,
As cross the Earth we wandered then observing pain and grief,
To witness all the trials and troubles that cruel men have fashioned,
And all the sorrows of men's strife that we were bound to meet.

Canto Five

Conducted by Urania on another aerial flight, the Voyager then
bears witness to the world as suffering. They there observe the
prejudice of men, and mankind's plight, and how the greed for power
and wealth destroys eventually. In this Urania seeks to show how
Hells arise from souls, through clinging to desires which blinds
attunement to the whole.

Rolling seas did lie before,
My body weak, my Lady sure,
She tended no respite, as out the desert's howling blasts,
Sands did scatter, cross wind storms,
Did moan as I spied distant forms,
Like half seen dreams, on distant shores,
Arising as we climbed.

We brave the daunting flight thence took,
Two mariners of the air,
Unsure of our direction, Or her goal, the whence, or where,
Until my Lady took the lead, through banks of mist and cloud,
Descending with a slowing pace, to reach some barren ground.

And there beneath a spreading bough, I did with shock and awe,
Observe a corpse of youthful form, left hanging from a tree,
its neck was broke, its breath expired, its body cut and stripped,
its arms displayed no force of life,
from working in the ditch-
as he had oft been forced to strive,
and oft been made to do.

(The Muse):
Here hangs a man,
no animal,
who forced to slavery,
Endured the loss,

of human rights,
denied his dignity,
and every basic civil right,
affording liberty.

Behold the head,
which you possess,
Evolved within,
the channels pressed,
The vault enfolded memory,
Of each genetic century,
He was your father, as thou art his brother family tied.

The blood which moved beneath his breast,
With pure free air, once flowed and bled,
All kin deserve their daily bread,
All human skin beneath is red:
He was your father, as thou art his brother family tied.

Thou art the body cosmic, and through this be family tied,
Let this true democratic law be lived and testified:
All human life be one, and in that one be unified,
Instate that law, for in that law, true justice be enshrined.

But bigots know not right from wrong, for blind they cannot see,
That colour tones of human beings should not denote the creed,
With hood and cross and lynching mob, they hang men in a tree,
As they expound cruel doctrines of a white supremacy.

No man or woman, youth or child, or any living thing,
Should be enforced to bondage, as a slave is to a king,
Oh wield your hearts, with faith be strong, be glad and joyous sing,
In dreams find consolation through the hope that freedom brings.

And as I stood and bent my head in sadness, mixed with shame,
A distant chorus filled my heart with Spirit's proud refrain.

(Chorus):
Oh one man's freedom fighter is an abolitionist,
And one man's freedom fighter is a segregationist,
And one man's freedom fighter is another's terrorist:
From Selma to the mighty walls of old Jerusalem.

And one man's freedom fighter is a man we all should know,
Who hides his face in hooded garb and sleeps with old Jim Crow,
Whilst other men he hates and kills toil for him in the fields:
From Selma to the mighty walls of old Jerusalem.

No Whiteman, Blackman, Gentile, Jew,
Men's freedom should deny,
Or bond with chains the hand to labour, justice to decry,
All human beings are equal born, and always should be free:
From Selma to the mighty walls of old Jerusalem.

Its cotton picking time again, the flowers are all in bloom,
The seeds a scatterin' on the wind, the harvesters in tune,
God's hand we seek, to bear our woes, whilst we pluck with our fingers,
As black skinned all, we be enslaved, hard toil is all that lingers:
From Selma to the mighty walls of old Jerusalem.

The colour tone of good men's skin should not support a claim,
Denote a mark of character, or force another's name,
To be adopted, or erased, for economic gain,
From Selma to the mighty walls of old Jerusalem.

Let good men not be prejudiced,
Nor slaves be bought or sold,
No price be placed on free men's heads,
No soul be bought with gold,
No human should be value priced,
And never should be owned,
From Selma to the mighty walls of Old Jerusalem.

A king upon a mountain top proclaimed a noble dream,
So all who laboured and did thirst,
should drink from freedom's stream,

So free at last they too might cross,
the river Babylon,
Till by the shore, they weep no more,
as slaves for lost Zion.

As I gazed up, the thought did strike,
A bitter irony,
That swift drew out a parallel with wars from history,
That the Crusades, the Christian knights in arms, that slew the Kurd,
Had sown the seed to thus bequeath this present legacy.

The Spirit then recalled that once another man had hung,
Amidst some branching scaffolding, whilst grieving Mary sung,
The Psalm of Psalms, whilst Roman spears had sought to pierce his lung.

Reflecting on this truth, I then took comfort that the past,
was now no longer present in the faith that held me fast,
The past was not the present, but those trials had helped men see,
The evils of their actions, and had helped to set them free.

But as I sought to use the past as timely recompense,
To purge my heart of sorrow at the prejudice of men,
My Lady swift dispelled the thought and made a new defence,
By showing revelations that transcended such pretence.

(Muse):
Even in these present times there lives by cause of greed,
Despicable promotions which result in slavery,
Where children, men and women are still traded for a price,
For trafficking, forced marriage, or licentious sexual vice,
How poor addressed be those who cite injustices like these,
Rich men kill great ideals in pursuit of vanities!

Conducted by the Spirit's grace, she showed me by her favour,
Bore witness to the roots of greed and how by men's device,
The poor and frail are bought in sale, and bonded to their labour,
Whilst rich men's hands did plot and plan more wealth from unjust vice.

One girl I saw, by father maimed,
Was sold through contrived tears,
To all who sought a barter,
As his wailing filled my ears.

A woman too exploited was oft beaten and attacked,
Then found an occupation in a room upon a sack,
While pimps became her profiteers,
poor junkies broke her back.

From Kandahar to Old Lahore, the streets of blue Bangkok,
The traders leave their poppy seeds stashed in the poor sweatshops,
The flowers trade as images,
as war's Forget-me-nots,
Yet form to crave, benumb to save,
life's painful influence.

In hashish tents, the Bedouin tribes, who from Jabal Burdah,
Do wind across the desert dunes,
by meteor and star,
Preach their trade as heroes,
whilst in hallowed marbled halls,
They seek to trap the infidel,
before great Allah's call.

More martyrs for the needs of men addicted,
than the law:
they pledge their holy troth to God with tears,
their faith adorned,
But not upon the sepulchres of those who bled and fought,
Who gave their lives for peace;
Let peace with prayer not tears be sought. [1]

The Spirit then raised up mine eyes to distant mountain peaks,
Where I did see before me all the histories of mankind,

---

[1] **Opium** (poppy tears, lachryma papaveris) is the dried latex obtained from the poppy (Papaver somniferum).

Stretching out before me were weird panoramic scenes,
Of war and death and poverty throughout the centuries.

And leading from the front was Death in flowing hooded garb,
Astride her steed Apocalypse, as plague broke in her wake,
And close behind the Foolish King, half stripped of flesh and blood,
Who led his subjects tied by chains with sickening dignity.

Emperors, merchants, tramps and thieves, and every class and station,
Did writhe and groan, with ghastly tones, imbued by their life acts,
As if their states of consciousness held karmic consequences,
And each and every thought and deed enforced some secret pact,
Which had been drawn without their prior agreement of the fact.

The artists too that I had met made up the company,
Reciting verse of dreadful scenes with anguished irony,
Which added to the pathos of this circus tragedy.

(Muse):
The least rejected spirit kept on Earth,
Devours great ribs of gold to cause the birth,
Of wars and vile pollutions, ever rife,
Whilst claiming it can buy the better life.

Its servants idolise and downward bend,
To covet and aspire to betterment,
Whilst those who through their indexed price extend,
Makes ill gained profits, buying government.

Whilst popes and priests do claim true wealth resides,
In heaven, whilst they earthly wealth despise:
Place treasure up in heaven, goods reduct,
For earth with moth and rust too soon corrupt.

(The Voyager cynically):
A rouse no more to keep the masses quiet,
To curb the revolution and the riot,
Whilst they, the Church, aspire to own the gold,
Which separates the rich man from the fold.

How can a camel thread the needle's eye?
How may a rich man enter paradise?
Ye may not both be pious and replete,
With gold or treasure, 'tis not right nor meet;
By that poor stance, rich churchmen oft do speak,
Yet have not often practised what they preach!

But each soul needs fair pay for honest labours,
And not the tax of Church Indulgences,
Mitigating tithes for heaven's favours,
Are reap`ed not through great divulgences.

(Muse):
Yet there be virtue in good toil and labour,
Honest trade deserves our honest praise,
Every kindly deed brings virtue's favour,
Helps the human race traverse the ways.

Happiness is deemed in life a pleasure,
Pleasure oft is cast from goods or gold,
Happiness requires a certain measure,
Something more than what is bought and sold.

Beauty, love and reason are eternal,
Only we shall change and pass away,
Value rests not in our wealth external,
But if we from virtue's path did stray.

(Urania exhorting):
Practise living virtues for mankind,
Not for gifts bestowed in paradise,
Sharing shall ensure the heritage,
So that humankind rewarded is.

Measured wealth lies not in products owned,
But how we our actions do address,
Honest, true affections, fairly shown,
By degrees of virtue may be blessed.

And through moderate practise we may grow,
And through temperance we true riches own,
Noble friends, live modest lives from birth,
Do not seek to prejudice the earth.

(Her voice begins to fade and change into many others):
Practise living virtues for mankind,
Not for pleasures born in paradise,
Live and share, ensure the heritage,
So our children's legacy may live.

(The Voyager):
Is there no reward in suffering?
I my strange companion did address,
As I stood still fearful and bereft,
Of my courage lingering over death,
Whilst strange visions passed on either side,
Wailing on their losses as they cried.

(Muse):
Trials you see are nought but shades and forms,
Phantoms born from your reality,
By your inner mind they come to be,
Can'st thou not distinguish what thou sees?

If men do believe this truth shall pass,
And their present deeds they don't amend:
Then these wailing ghosts that cling and gnash,
Shall true live, determined as an end.

As the frightful visions faded fast,
My sweet Lady's hand a lyre then grasped,
Strummed the strings, and with a noble voice,
Sung of perils summoned by free choice.

The Muse:
(singing an ascending and descending scale)
Strum the strings that stretch across the lyre,

So the soul's attunement is acquired,
By the modal tones that life inspires,
Played and practised by experience.

Songs fulfil the heart that strong desires,
Happiness and friendship, and aspires,
To the virtues that the soul requires,
As it loves, thence by good love it sings.

For the scale of life, a symphony,
May evolve from virtue's harmony,
If not then a strange cacophony,
May the scale of life accompany.

If false notes displace the melody,
And the tune be lost by vanity,
Seek good metre, not disharmony,
Found in rhythms' regularity.

Oft transposed by life, in many keys,
Sing refrains of virtue's parity,
Lest the soul be struck by malady.
Keep good metre, not unmetered tones.

Let good virtue's needs be to the fore,
So the staves be fast and strongly shored,
Pon the bedrock of the lower cleft,
Thence to be augmented as is best.

Craving wealth as goods or luxuries,
Should not quell desires for purer needs,
Give the best required to fill the heart,
And the joy of happiness impart.

Love is so elusive to define,
Harder still to practise or refine,
Priceless in its value, e'er sublime,
It enriches both our hearts and minds.

Love alone makes human life complete,
Whilst desires for luxuries defeat,
Love shall bless, and through sweet joy emplaced,
Fill the heart, and sorrows there replace.

Oft desires for endless products wrought,
Are the mark of good societies,
Which proclaim they are both sold and bought,
In the interests of propriety.

For their ownership be civilised,
And the one's that shirk, must good work lack,
Thence without a wage they are despised,
Those that bear no labour, bear no craft,
So their virtues are ill recognised,
Cast in terms of wealth that work defines.

Yet in striving, avarice and greed,
Breeds a yield of thrice polluting seeds,
Spoiling Earth, and spoiling minds and hearts,
Marring soul, they reap disparity;
So desire from love, the nobler part,
Must from goodness' company depart.

Pleasure may be found in ownership,
And in honest trade a goodly life,
But if gold or gift be coveted,
That a detriment shall virtue's blight.
This then is the Hell on Earth Man bears,
which all through their greed shall recreate,
It resides not in the fiery bowels,
Of the Earth where demons foul prostrate,

There before their Lord in revelries,

Writhing 'midst black blood and effigies.

All in all such striving yields no more,
When by passage we must leave the shore,
In the end, all striving must be left:
None require such needs in facing death.

Then my Lady calm, with voice assured,
Spoke of how in life death is abjured:

All things born in nature pass away,
Death is hard, but take thy comfort still,
Time that ruinous flow shall have its way,
Though fair loves be lost, pain has its day.

Pain of loss be ebbing like the tide,
Tears of loss that grieveth yield to sighs,
Hearts shall be redeemed, Pray do not cry,
E'er derive consoling memories.

Life will bring hard trials, but do not weep,
Bear thy sorrow, and protect thy kin,
Bear your children's hopes and dreams to keep,
Bear thy tears in private kept within,
In the confines of your secret thoughts,
Let your sorrows not your heart destroy,
Ever tending nurture there the joy,
So thy heart in love be truly steeped.

All things shall arise and pass away,
Be not fearful of a bitter end,
Gladly keep a light and happy heart,
And be troubled not by foe or friend.

Keep the joy of life, a pleasure sacred,
Tend thou not the roots of vice or hatred,
Fear of death in living blights the day,
On death's day there be no debt to pay.

Death is but a friend, no enemy,
Bound with life it brings true parity;
Cloaks life's pain, with peace and harmony,
Thence redressed new life begins again.

Death is but the shadow of creation,
Balances the living animation,
Rest within its peace filled sublimation,
Till the process be reborn again.

Canto Six

The Voyager is conducted to the outer realms of Earth,
before departing to the centre of the universe. Urania accompanies
to guide and then explain the nature of the sun and stars which form
the Milky Way.

By truth revealed,
in visions rare,
I came to realise,
That life and death,
were intertwined,
within my Lady's eyes,

I knew within,
the anima,
my joy and fears were framed,
And knew within,
the animus,
my shadow self remained,
I knew that she,
and I were one,
Reflected, parts of soul,
Reformed by Spirit, unified,
Recast in part and whole.

I knew the shades that I had seen had no substantial form,
But were, but mere projections from my inner faculties,
I felt the love within me grow, whilst on the orbit's plane,
I sought to look before me, as my Spirit spoke again.

(Muse):
May Justice as a virtue light the heart, and fill the mind,
Let Justice be the measure of equality, and bind,

The soul to understanding of its place in wisdom's scheme,
So universal suffrage, truth and freedom be achieved.

Practise virtue's, love and know, and as you strive, be kind,
And occupy the heart's desires, with friendship, truth define,
Assimilate this life, and by this enterprise sublime,
The essence of thy soul shall by the cosmos be refined.

And if your love be pure, it shall project you to the stars,
And if your heart is selfless, then your soul shall be set free,
And if your love is good and pure, you shall be free to roam,
Amongst the stars, and find the path which surely leads you home,
Back to the place from whence you came,
And where you ought to be.

My Lady then did speak to me of yet one more adventure,
Whilst seeking to assure me, and assuage my growing fear,
With calming reassurance that evoked no pain or censure,
She wove a revelation,
That unlocked life's mystery.

(Muse):
Hatch out hopes in voyages to explore,
Vistas deep and to the breach once more,
Muster brave the courage to endure:
Auto theos agape estin.

Men oft use this mantra as a shield,
Keeping fear well hidden in their hearts,
But we must not 'til we with our eyes,
See the place wherein which God resides.

Timelessness achieved is yet unknown,
Hours and minutes are in space dethroned,
Time that king of life shall have its basis,
Subject to the flight's velocity.

Now my love embrace this vision shared,
For ye now shall age not as we dare,

We shall swift betray the centuries.
As we flee from Time concurrently.

Whilst all life on Earth shall pass away,
As all things must pass, we shall not be,
subject to the work of night and day,
We shall seem to live eternally.

Three dimensions that we now can see,
Lead us to the fourth, and presently,
Other realms which to the heart inclined,
Shall be accessed by the soul aligned.

Herculean pillars on the edge,
Of the astral fields we shall rebuke,
Crystal spheres and mists ethereal,
Shall not occupy our wandering minds.

Nor shall occult tracts on chemistry,
Drawn from magic mirror clouds be scried,
Nor shall we in alchemy lay hope,
Nor lend trust to false astrology.

Not through faith, but science shall we linger,
Nor through faith in blind deductive schema,
But the grounds of logic and induction,
Gathered to our hearts precipitously.

For through sense and every mathematic,
Shall the views before us be made clear,
So that false beliefs in gods and angels,
From men's dreaming hearts may thus be purged.

(The Voyager):
If there be dimensions more than this,
Which access to souls alone are made,
Let me not be blind or prejudiced,
Lest I spurn salvation in the grave.

But until the psychic eye can see,
I shall not displace my dignity,
Reasoning the truth to know no fear,
So that then the cosmic face be clear.

And if I, through error, lose the pathway,
Shall I through false knowledge thus be damned?
As a Satan purged of power for wisdom,
Or an Adam punished for a plan?

They like God through knowledge sought to conquer,
Innocence and love were not enough,
Jealous of their power, God thus condemned them,
Hence both they and God became corrupt!

(Muse):
Stories such as these through sense and reason,
Are when analysed still lacking proof,
Banished from the garden not from Eden,
Which is just a metaphor for youth.

Eden is our planet seed of nature,
and in this the cosmos is the womb,
So we must now set out on the journey,
To return to where we once were born.

Canto Seven

The Canticle of Departure.

Travelling at a speed unknown,
the swift velocities,
Did span the space we then embraced,
as if the clarity,
Of mind and body played its part,
as like was drawn to like:
The light within our hearts embraced the light within the stars.

We did not lose our faith, or fear the void betwixt the light,
But knew that we would soon be free,
to trace our path in flight,
and from thenceforth our souls would seek
the true reality.

And as the stars illuminating,
Cast their energy,
The Spirit sought to then explain the nature of their being.

(Muse):
Within the heart of every star a core of hydrogen,
Will synthesise its atoms, fuse, and then form helium,
And this creative process causes heat and energy,
Irradiating solar light to cause all life to be.

The hydrogen exhausted must result in helium,
Which marries with its self-same form to yield a greater sum,
And thence, with helium consumed, the elemental sun,
Shall fuse anew and thus produce resulting oxygen.

Such is the lifespan of the stars,
For all that lives must die,
A billion worlds evolve within the blinking of an eye.

The stars turn not the wheels of Fate, But turn upon their axis,
Combusting proton fusion with abundant hydrogen,
Explode extending filaments, the streams, a natural praxis,
Emit atomic particles, coroneal, as one.

The solar wind beyond the fringe of Pluto's orb expanding,
Cocoons the planet seeds within the sphere of Helios,
Bombarding the ionosphere, magnetic fields colliding,
Inducing with transparent veils expanding joyousness.

Aurora on the throne of Night,
Draws praise and exclamations,
From those who from the coils of sleep,
unfettered now observe,
To offer with her crown of light,
electric excitations,
Repaid with thrift the homage of their hearts' solicitude.

Yet she must flee like vapour mists, to melt, although delighting,
To be replaced by sombre cloud, the vaulted troposphere,
To slip concealed beyond the morn, and with the sun alighting,
Reborn she rises, dissipates, beneath the exosphere.

The sisters of the Pleiades, the Pillars of Creation,
The coloured cloud of nebulae protect in nurseries,
The young evolving planet spheres,
Which house the life formations,
To nurture rich organic soup,
to feed life's chemistry.

The cosmic light which there reflects a sense of prearrangement,
Is but the source of life through chance, and process formed in stars,
No light of mind, no light of God, will blind us to estrangement,
Distract us with illusions and confusions of the heart.

There are no hosts, angelic choirs, no ringing horns apparent,
No Sybil saints to orchestrate the price that we must pay,
No kabbalah, zikhron teruah, accompany defiant,
No gates of Heaven, nor of Hell, to block our wing'ed way.

Speeding through the lanes of dust which form the Milky Way,
Traversing swift Centaurus' arm, we did not go astray,
We flew towards the centre formed by Sagittarius,
And in that place I did not hear God's strange cacophony.

(Muse):
Ye shall not waves magnetic hear,
Such waves evade the ear,
My Lady spoke, as I invoked, a prayer to ease my fear.

(Muse):
Electro waves magnetic may transverse then fade away,
Such waves so strange hath not the range, but ne'er shall they decay.

Yet as I felt the Muse's words no comfort did they send,
Of who she was and who was I?
Where would this journey end?
I felt my end was part of her,
But why I did not know,
The fear did creep, and burrow deep, within my mortal soul.

(The Voyager):
Oh why do we swift flee from that which is the source of life?
And why do we with daunting speed embrace the frozen night?
Towards the very centre of that luminous galaxy,
Within its starless heart, wherein no life, nor light can be!

(Muse):
That starless heart was once a star, and as a star gave birth,
To interstellar matter formed to make a universe:
Black Star of Death, a mighty force, that consumes energy,
Your dreadful might shall drink the light, and draw all things to thee!

This said I knew I clung to Death,
My soul I recognised,
Within her gaze, my eyes did range,
Yet still her love I spied;
Such love did quell my fears and pain, to cause my woe to cease,
negating a death struggle,
as I slowly felt at peace.

Until her folded pinioned wings,
Held fast to suffocate,
My weaken'ed form, until forlorn,
all strength had ebbed from me.

~

Communio
A muse is but an angel,
a higher faculty,
Which must as part of soul submit to brief mortality,
Yet underlying life exists the primal energy,
A spirit force, which e'er endures, and caused all things to be.

As onwards ever onwards the procession of the stars,
Did shine with spirit's power immense,
a radiant legacy,
No beating wings, no air did bring,
No sound or melody,
As spirit flew beyond the depths,
Of soul's mortality . . .

Sic transit gloria mundi,
Sic transit hominem,
Incipit vita nova,
Thus ends the requiem.

CPSIA information can be obtained at www.ICGtesting.com
Printed in the USA
LVOW11*1921101016

508158LV00019B/557/P